Living with Mom, Spending Time with Dad

Colleen H Robley-Blake

Order this book online at www.trafford.com
or email orders@trafford.com

Most Trafford titles are also available at major online book retailers.

 www.trafford.com

North America & international
toll-free: 844 688 6899 (USA & Canada)
fax: 812 355 4082

Our mission is to efficiently provide the world's finest, most comprehensive book publishing service, enabling every author to experience success. To find out how to publish your book, your way, and have it available worldwide, visit us online at www.trafford.com

Because of the dynamic nature of the Internet, any web addresses or links contained in this book may have changed since publication and may no longer be valid. The views expressed in this work are solely those of the author and do not necessarily reflect the views of the publisher, and the publisher hereby disclaims any responsibility for them.

Any people depicted in stock imagery provided by Getty Images are models, and such images are being used for illustrative purposes only.
Certain stock imagery © Getty Images.

Illustrations Copyright 2009 by Imaajinn This

Illustrated by Randy Jennings

ISBN: 978-1-4269-1612-0 (sc)
      978-1-4669-2504-5 (e)

Library of Congress Control Number: 2009936399

Print information available on the last page.

Trafford rev. 03/04/2021

Thanks

God
Nothing is ever possible without you.

Stephen & Alex
I could never do this without you.   Love you both.

Mom & Vanessa
For all your feedback, e-mails and phone calls.

Steve
Thank you for sharing your story with me.

Thanks to everyone for all the love and support.

I saw my dad packing his bag as he continued to shout,
While mom kept yelling for him to get out!
I couldn't help but wonder, "What was the driving force?
Why did Mom and Dad decide to get a divorce?"

I pleaded with my mom, "Please don't let Dad go."

She said, "I'm sorry Alex, but it has to be so.

Our arguing and screaming isn't good for you and your brother.

The constant fighting is making us hate each other.

Sometimes a divorce can be a mess.

However, it doesn't mean you're loved any less.

Even though your father and I argue, fuss, and fight.

Everything will eventually be alright."

Mom's reassuring words didn't help me much.
How am I supposed to deal with this stuff?
I feel like the only kid experiencing this mess.
Who could I talk to and confess?

I really miss my dad, I wish it wasn't so.
Why does he have to go?

I remember when we were a happy family.
We played games, watched movies, and were just goofy.

Riding our bikes in the bright summer sun,
We would scream, laugh, and have so much fun.
Everyone got along.
Something must have gone terribly wrong.

Dad would chase us up and down the beach.
While Mom relaxed and ate a peach.

When Mom cooked dinner Stephen and I would fight.

We each wanted to serve Dad every night.

We would take food and a drink straight to Dad.

He would wink at us and say, "Don't forget the ketchup little lads."

Mom and Dad would hug and kiss.

It was nice to see so much bliss.

They would utter, "I love you," to each other.

Dad would proudly say, "I'm glad I decided to marry your mother."

Mom would always shriek with joy and laughter.

Things were so much better before, than they were after.

Every night Dad would tell us bedtime stories.
About trucks, airplanes, and chocolate candies.
Some nights after saying our prayers,
Stephen and I would fall asleep curled up on the chairs.

Dad would smile and put down his coffee cup.
Very gently, he would pick us up.
He would put us in bed and tuck us in real tight.
While he showered us with hugs and kisses before saying,

Goodnight.

I don't understand why this has to be.
Why can't we stay together as a family?
Living with Mom and spending time with Dad.
That's not the way I had it planned; I feel so mad.

Then I thought about the times when I heard them fight.

They would say things to each other that just weren't right.

Did they not see Stephen and I sitting there?

Or had they forgotten how to care?

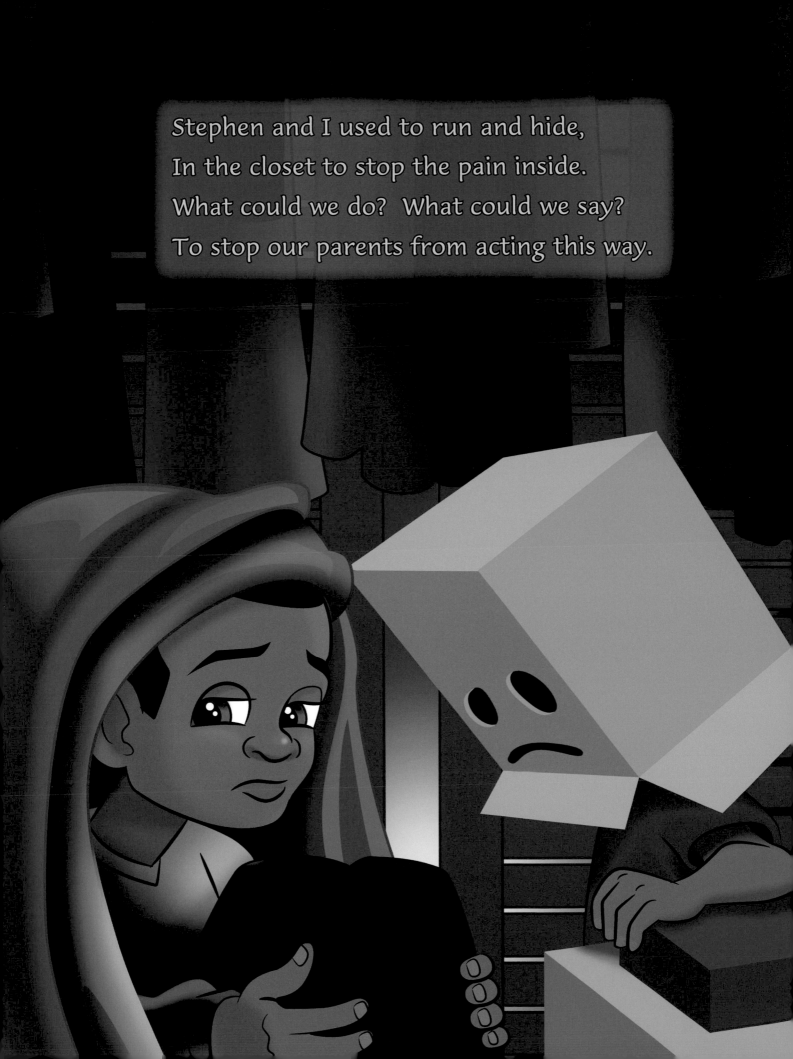

Even though the fighting was worse than before,
After a while we didn't run and hide anymore.
Stephen would cover his ears and sit on the floor,
Screaming, "Please Mom and Dad, I can't take anymore."

I looked at Mom and Dad with tears in my eyes.
While each of them yelled, "Stop telling lies!"
I thought Mom loved Dad and he loved her back.
Was that how love made people act?

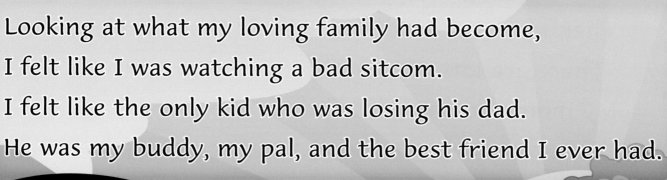

Looking at what my loving family had become,
I felt like I was watching a bad sitcom.
I felt like the only kid who was losing his dad.
He was my buddy, my pal, and the best friend I ever had.

Then Mom sat me down and said that wasn't so.
"There are lots of kids whose fathers had to go.
My mom and dad got a divorce too.

Everything my mom said to me at that time came true.

Don't think you are the only ones feeling blue.

There are other kids just like Stephen and you.

Look at me, I turned out fine.

My mom was there for me all the time.

My dad wasn't there, but yours will always be.

He loves you and Stephen unconditionally.

So even though he has left, you can see him whenever.

He'll love you and Stephen forever and ever."

I sat there with a sad look on my face.
Without my dad, my house was an empty place.
My mom and dad did get a divorce.
I didn't feel good about it of course.

Presents from Mom and gifts from Dad-
Even money from Grandma couldn't stop me from feeling sad.

I hadn't seen Stephen like this before—no, never.
He really missed Dad more than ever.
He slammed the doors and yelled a lot.
I thought his uncontrollable crying would never stop.
But I think the only thing wrong with Stephen and I,
Was the missing link in our family.

SLAM!

MILK

My mom said she knew a boy just like me.

He lives with his dad Steve, and spends time with his mommy.

So when my mom says, "Alex, it's time for bed."

I imagine Steve saying, "Son, come let's read."

After a few months I didn't feel so blue.
Everything my mom said really came true.
My dad loves Stephen and I unconditionally.
We're still a family despite living separately.
We can visit him whenever we choose.
Stephen and I have nothing to lose.

He remembers to pick us up on Fridays.
He's always around; especially for birthdays and holidays.

Spending time with Dad is such a blast.

I wish this cool time could really last.

I get to enjoy things twice as much.

The presents are doubled for birthdays, Christmas, and such.

At the end of the weekend I get extremely sad,
When I have to leave my dad.
Living with Mom and spending time with Dad,
Has now made me happier and less sad.

Sometimes I hear my mom cry when she thinks I'm asleep.

When I'm with my dad he tosses and turns in his sleep.

The divorce has also changed their lives.

They're no longer like other husbands and wives.

I know Mom and Dad were once birds of a feather.
Maybe someday they'll get back together.

I'll ask Stephen for his help,
I know I can't do it by myself.
I want my parents back together and no longer tearful.
It's the only thing to make me permanently cheerful.

So every night I say a special prayer.
For Stephen, myself, and other kids out there.

When I close my eyes I always pray:
"Please let tomorrow be a better day.
I want you Lord to let Mom and Dad see,
A winning team is a family.
But until that time when they reunite,
Keep them safe throughout the night.

To all the kids like me who suffer in pain.
Stay strong, I promise you things will get better again."

Living With Mom, Spending Time With Dad

My Name is

Have you or anyone you know experienced their parent's divorce?

What advice would you give to Alex to help him cope?

Living With Mom, Spending Time With Dad

Reading Exercise

Who is the main character in the story?

What problem does the main character face?

How does the story begin?

Why do you think Alex's parents are getting a divorce?

Living With Mom, Spending Time With Dad

Reading Exercise

Is Alex happy about his parents' decision to get a divorce?

How did Alex feel when his Mom and
Dad decided to get a divorce?

How did Alex feel when his Mom and Dad were fighting?

Did Stephen handle his parents' divorce better than Alex?

Living With Mom, Spending Time With Dad

Reading Exercise

Was Alex's parents ever happy together?

How did Alex feel when his Mom and Dad were happy?

Besides Alex, who else was missing their dad?

Why did Stephen and Alex hide in the closet?

Living With Mom, Spending Time With Dad

Reading Exercise

What makes birthdays and Christmas more special for Alex?

What did Alex's Mom say to him to make him feel better?

Why did Alex's parents want him to go see the doctor?

What did Alex's parents and grandma do to help him feel better?

Living With Mom, Spending Time With Dad

Reading Exercise

Why do you think Alex did not like the presents
from his parents and his grandma?

\---

\---

Why would Alex be happy if his parents got back together?

\---

\---

Do you think Stephen and Alex can get
their parents back together?

\---

\---

How long did it take Alex to stop feeling sad?

\---

\---

Living With Mom, Spending Time With Dad

Reading Exercise

Do you think Alex is still sad?

Do you think Alex would be happy again?

What advice would you give to Alex to help him cope?

How do you feel about the story?

Printed in the United States
by Baker & Taylor Publisher Services